799.1

# Contents

# Are you going fishing today?

Mark's hobby is fishing. In the summer holidays, he goes fishing nearly every day. One morning at breakfast, he gets a shock. His cousin Emma is coming to stay. Emma's dad has given her some money to buy a fishing rod. She wants to go fishing with Mark.

3

# The tackle

5

# Rods and reels

## Rods

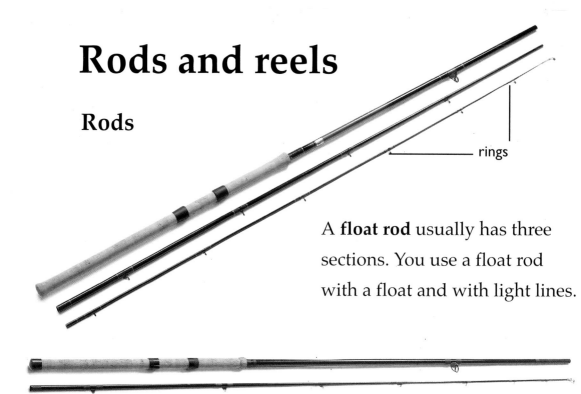

rings

A **float rod** usually has three sections. You use a float rod with a float and with light lines.

A **leger rod** is shorter than a float rod.

A leger rod usually has two sections.

You use a leger rod with weights.

---

**TIPS**

- Buy the best rod you can.
- Choose a rod made of hollow fibreglass or carbon fibre. These are light.
- Buy the longest float rod you can handle.

- Don't buy a 'junior rod'.
- Don't buy a rod with a wooden or a plastic handle. They slip and don't last. Rods with cork or foam handles are better.

# Reels

Don't buy a cheap reel. You need a good reel that works smoothly. Ask the tackle dealer to say which reel is best for you.

bale arm
(guide for line)

**open-faced reel**
*Best reel for general use*

spool

slipping clutch
(adjusts the amount of line)

## closed-faced reel

*Covered design stops line tangle. Good for fishing in a wind.*

Make sure the winder is OK for you.
**Right-handed people**
You need a winder on the LEFT-hand side.
**Left-handed people**
You need a winder on the RIGHT-hand side.

# Getting ready

When are we going fishing?

Mark!

Not today.

That's right, ruin my holiday. I'm not a baby-sitter.

No, but you have to look after Emma today, because I'm going out. Did you buy anything at the tackle shop?

Yes, I got some line and a reel. OK, OK, I get the message. We'll go fishing!

Can we go now? I'm ready.

No, you're not. Go and put some jeans on, and change out of that bright T-shirt.

Later...

# Where can you fish ?

pond

lake

You can fish for freshwater fish in still waters or in running water.

gravel pit

reservoir

stream

*Streams can be good to fish in after rain.*

## Close Season

In most areas there is a Close Season when you can't fish. Fish breed at this time. Ask your local tackle dealer if there's a Close Season in your area.

## Licences and permits

You need a rod licence to fish in your area. You may need a permit as well. Clubs and land-owners will sell you permits.

## Clubs

It's a good idea to join a fishing club. Clubs look after most water in England and Wales. Club members pay less for permits. You meet other keen anglers at clubs as well.

river

*Some rivers are fast-flowing. Others have slow-moving water.*

# Do's and don'ts

## Do

Keep away from the edges of banks. They may be slippery or steep.
▼

▲
Shut gates behind you, and don't walk through crops.

## Don't

Don't be a litter lout. Take your litter home with you.

Keep your tackle close to you, and away from people and  animals.

▼

▲

Keep quiet. Fish can hear voices and music. They can hear feet walking on the bank, too.

Don't wade without checking how deep the water is. Never wade in very fast-flowing water. Watch out for holes.

# Choosing a swim

Let's go and fish over there. There are other people fishing there.

You can't set up beside other anglers. They don't like it. Anyway this is a better place.

Why is it a better place? It's all the same river, isn't it?

Yes, but if we don't choose a good swim, we won't catch anything. Fish go where they can find food.

What's a swim?

It's the area of water where you fish.

14

"This is a good place. It's shady. Some fish like feeding in dark places."

"I can see some fish swimming down there. Look!"

"Yes. Fish like feeding in tree roots as well."

"Do fish ever swim near the surface?"

"Yes. They swim near the surface on hot days. Watch, keep quiet, and you'll see them."

"The anglers on the other bank are fishing in the weeds."

"They're fishing for pike. Pike like weedy places."

# Tackle

**Rods, and carrying case**

## Reel

Choose a reel with two spools
if you can. You can put light
lines on one spool, and heavy
lines on the other one.

*reel and spool*

## Line

You need more than one line.
Big, heavy fish are strong, and
you need a strong line to hold
them. You need a lighter line
for smaller fish.

## Floats and float box

You need wagglers for still-water fishing, and for slow water on a river. Stick floats are for running water.

## Leger weights

This type are called Arlesey bombs. They come in different sizes. You use them to hold the line in the right place.

## Split shot for float fishing

These come in different weights. You use them to hold the float in the right place.

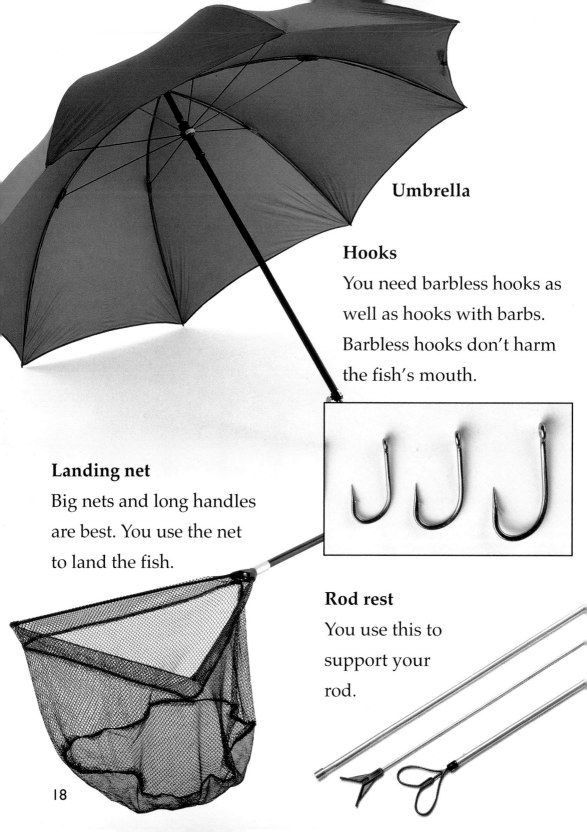

**Umbrella**

**Hooks**

You need barbless hooks as well as hooks with barbs. Barbless hooks don't harm the fish's mouth.

**Landing net**

Big nets and long handles are best. You use the net to land the fish.

**Rod rest**

You use this to support your rod.

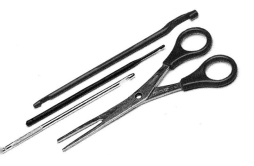

## Hook disgorger and forceps

These are for removing the hook from the fish's mouth.

### TIPS

• Buy good tackle. It is expensive to buy poor tackle as you have to replace it more often.

• Ask your tackle dealer for advice.

• Buy the right tackle for the job. The line and reel for pike fishing are not the same as for trout fishing.

**Bait container**

## Keep net

You use this to keep your fish if you need to. Never keep a fish in it for long.

# Setting up

Do you take it out now?

I take out the centre section, yes. Then I fit it to the butt section ... the rings have to line up, see?

Now draw the bag off the rod. If you do it like this, the different sections of the rod don't bang against each other.

Now I put the reel on.

Do you put it on the end?

No, it goes as far up the handle as it can. If you put the reel at the end, the rod is top-heavy.

# Where to find your fish

There are many types of fish in a river. Not all fish like the same part of the river.

**Overhanging bushes**
*Chub like shadowy water.*
*Barbel like it in the shadows if the water is fast.*

**Lilies**
*Bream and pike like lilies.*

**Slack water**
*Roach and pike like it here.*

**Slow water above weir**
*Roach and bream like it here.*

**Fast water below weir**
*Barbel like deep, fast areas.*

Fast, deep water on narrow bend
*Barbel and chub like it here.*

Slow, deep water on wide bend
*Roach and chub swim here.*

Shallow eddies
*Nearly all fish like these.*

Deep eddies
*Roach and bream swim here,*
*so do perch and pike.*

Tree roots from fallen tree
*Chub and barbel feed here as long as*
*the water is fast.*

23

# On the bank

What are you fishing for?

Chub. Don't speak so loudly. Chub are shy. You'll frighten them away.

What does a chub look like?

It's got a big head and a big mouth and it's got thick lips.

What colour is it?

It's got a dark back, with big silver and bronze scales. Its tail fin is black round the edges. The lower fins are red.

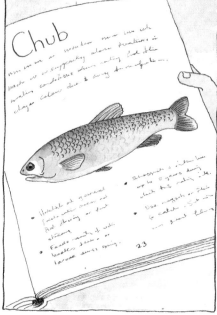

25

# Know your fish

 **Barbel** Sometimes called 'Old Whiskers' because it has four long barbels on its long snout.

 **Bream** It has a deep body. Its lips jut out. Bream are silver when young. Then they go bronze-brown.

 **Carp** It has a thick, deep body and four barbels. It is a greeny-brown fish.

 **Chub** It has a big head and mouth, and one fin on its back. Its scales are silver and bronze.

 **Dace** A slim fish, with a small, silvery body. Its fins are usually pink.

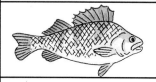 **Perch** It has two fins on top. One is spiky. There are stripes down each side. The lower fins are bright orange or red.

 **Roach** A streamlined fish with silvery scales. It has a dark back, orange-red eyes and a small mouth.

 **Trout** It can be brown or silver. It has black or coloured rings and spots.

 **Pike** A wicked fish! It is big, with teeth like a shark. It has green and yellow patterns on its body.

| Fast rivers | Slow rivers | Large lakes and reservoirs | Gravel pits | Quiet lakes and ponds | Canals |
|---|---|---|---|---|---|
| ✓ | | | | | |
| | ✓ | ✓ | ✓ | ✓ | ✓ |
| | ✓ | | ✓ | ✓ | |
| ✓ | ✓ | | | | |
| ✓ | | | | | |
| | ✓ | ✓ | ✓ | ✓ | ✓ |
| | ✓ | ✓ | ✓ | ✓ | ✓ |
| ✓ | ✓ | ✓ | ✓ | ✓ | |
| | ✓ | ✓ | ✓ | | |

# Checking the depth

# Float fishing and legering

## Float fishing

You use a long rod for float fishing. The float is fixed to your line and bobs on the surface of the water. The line below the float is weighed down by pieces of shot. When the fish takes the bait, it pulls the float down, so you know you've got a bite.

### FLOATS

The tops of floats are painted. Choose the colour that you can see best on the water. Good colours are black, orange, red, white and yellow.

The bottom of the float can be white, brown, grey or green. These colours are good camouflage colours. Some floats are transparent, so the fish cannot see the part that goes under the water.

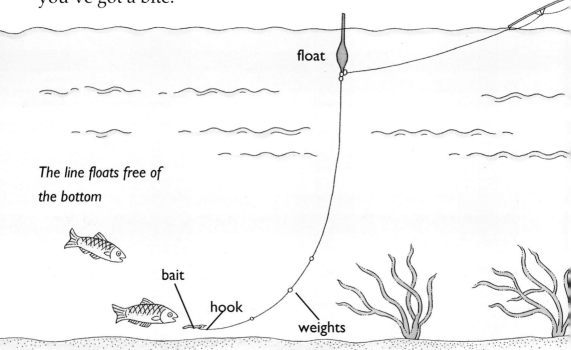

float

*The line floats free of the bottom*

bait

hook

weights

# Leger fishing

You can do leger fishing in still or running water. With legering, you keep the bait on the bed of the lake or river. You weigh the line down with a leger weight, such as the Arlesey bomb.

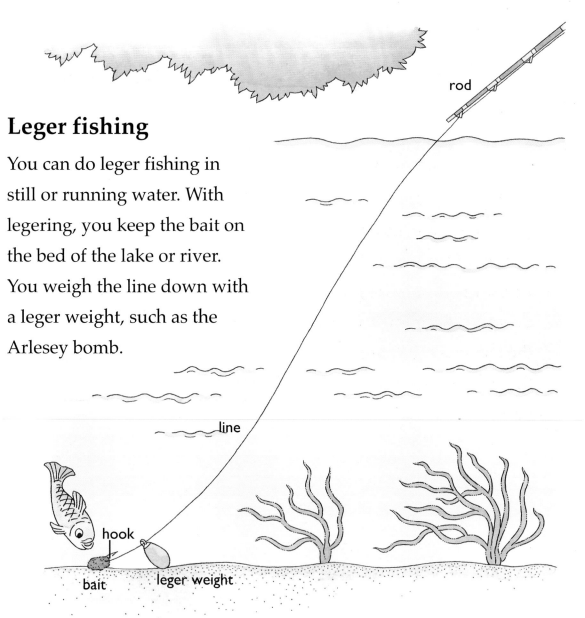

*The leger weight holds the line on the bottom.*

Leger fishing is very good for getting a bait to places where it isn't easy to cast, such as under bushes.

# Wriggly things

# Bait

## Wriggly bait

maggots     slugs

worms     caterpillars

insects

Keep your live bait in a bait container, with air holes in the lid.

## Kitchen bait

luncheon meat     bread

bacon     potato

sausage     cheese

sweetcorn     fruit

Make a paste from stale bread mixed with water. Add flavour by mixing in ripe bananas, cheese spread, drinking chocolate, honey or yeast.

# Grains

hempseed        tares

wheat             birdseed

wheat

Note: Hempseed is banned in some areas. Check your permit to find out if it is banned in your area.

birdseed

# Ground-bait

Ground-bait is used to attract fish to the place where you are fishing. It can float down through the water, or sit on the bottom. Ground-bait is usually made from stale bread mixed with water. Milk powder and egg shells are good for light ground-bait which drifts through the water. Make heavy ground-bait with bread, potato and some of the hook bait you are going to use.

# Careful!

37

# Hooks

Hooks come in sizes from 2(the largest) to 26 (the smallest).

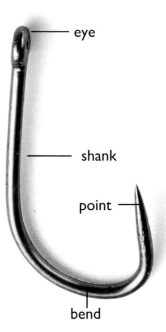

eye

shank

point

bend

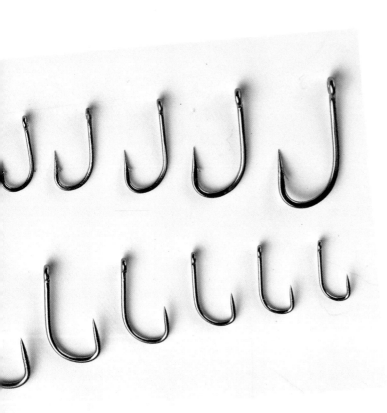

Micro barb hooks are best for wriggling baits like worms. Barbless hooks are best for other baits.

Make sure the hook point goes right through your bait. If you cover the hook point with bait, i won't catch in the fish's mouth.

# Casting

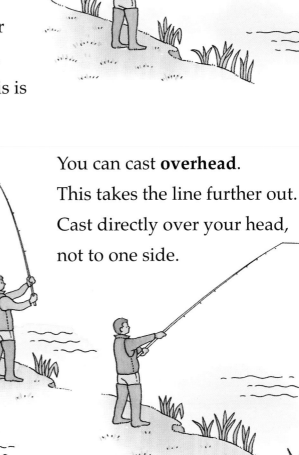

When you have baited your hook, you are ready to cast. You can cast **underarm**. This is the way to cast near to the bank.

You can cast **overhead**. This takes the line further out. Cast directly over your head, not to one side.

# Catching a fish

41

# Striking, playing, landing and returning

3 The fish fights back. The angler has to control the fish so it doesn't get away (playing).

▼
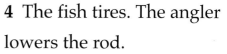

1 The fish bites.

4 The fish tires. The angler lowers the rod.

▼

▲

2 The line tightens as the angler pulls the rod. This fixes the hook in the fish's mouth (striking).

**5** Then the angler raises the rod to draw the fish into the landing net.

▼

▲

**7** The angler removes the hook from the fish's mouth.

▲

**6** The angler places the rod on the rod rest and takes the fish and landing net out of the water (landing).

▼

**8** The angler weighs and photographs the fish.

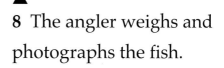

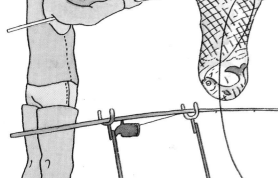

▲

**9** The angler carefully puts the fish back into the water (returning).

# Emma's turn

What happened?

You caught a tree! You shouldn't cast overhead near trees and bushes. And an underarm cast is better when you're fishing close to the bank.

Try again. That's better.

The float has gone, and something is pulling at the line.

Just pull a little, until you feel the fish.

# Fishy facts

Fish have ears. They can hear ▶ well in water. They can hear you from as far away as 12 metres. So keep quiet!

◀ Fish have very sharp eyes, and they can see all the way round. In daylight, they see in full colour. That means they can see your bright T-shirt and swim away. At night, and when the water is dark, fish see in black and white. Fish can't shut their eyes, because they do not have eyelids.

Fish have a very good sense of ▶
smell. They can smell food in
the water.

◀ Fish are fast. An average-sized
fish can swim at 16 miles per
hour!

Fish are cold-blooded, but ▶
they are very sensitive to
water temperature. They are
more lively when the water is
warm. They eat more when
they are more active. In cold
weather, they eat much less.

# Index